ALSO BY DAN CHIASSON

The Afterlife of Objects

Natural History

Natural History

POEMS

DAN CHIASSON

Alfred A. Knopf   New York   2007

Library of Congress Cataloging-in-Publication Data
Chiasson, Dan, [date]
Natural history / by Dan Chiasson.—1st ed.
p.   cm.
ISBN 978-0-375-71115-2
I. Title.
PS3603.H54N38 2005
811'.6—dc22
2005012416

Manufactured in the United States of America
Published October 11, 2005
First Paperback Edition, September 11, 2007

for Annie and Louis

Contents

II. Natural History

III.

Acknowledgments

Grateful acknowledgment to the editors of the following publications, where these poems, sometimes in different versions, first appeared:

Agni: "Natural History II (The Elephant)"

Boston Review: "Natural History VIII (Pliny)," "Natural History XII (Pliny II)," "Natural History XVIII ("There Is a Star in the Sea")"

Colorado Review: "Poem Beginning with a Line from Frost," "Natural History XXIV (The Soil)"

Lit: "Natural History XV (Randall Jarrell)"

Literary Imagination: "Natural History XXIII (Which Species on Earth Is Saddest?)"

Poetry: "Natural History I (The Sun)," "Natural History IV (The Hyenas)," "Four Horaces I (To Dan Chiasson Concerning Fortune)"

Slate: "Natural History V (The Bear)," "Natural History XI (Making Purple)," "'Scared by the Smallest Shriek of a Pig, and When Wounded, Always Give Ground'" (as "Frederick the Elephant")

TriQuarterly: "After Party," "Peeled Horse," "Natural History VII (Georgic)," "Natural History XIX (Georgic II)"

"Poem Beginning with a Line from Frost" appeared on *Poetry Daily* and in *Visiting Frost* (University of Iowa Press). "Natural History II (The Elephant)" appeared on *Verse Daily* and in the anthology *Legitimate Dangers: American Poets of the New Century* (Sarabande Books, 2006).

Time off to write this book was supported by Harvard University, by the Mrs. Giles Whiting Foundation and by the State University of New York, Stony Brook. My sincere thanks to them.

Thanks to the many friends who saw these poems in drafts. Special thanks to Deborah Garrison, Jeffrey Posternak and Frank Bidart.

I.

He wanted to feel the same way over and over.

—Wallace Stevens,
"This Solitude of Cataracts"

LOVE SONG (SMELT)

When I say "you" in my poems, I mean you.
I know it's weird: we barely met.
You must hear this all the time, being you.

That night we were at opposite ends of
the long table, after the pungent
Russian condiments, the carafes of tarragon vodka,

the chafing dishes full of boiled smelts
I was a little drunk: after you left,
I ate the last smelt off your dirty plate.

LOVE SONG (SYCAMORES)

Stop there, stop now, come no closer,
I said, but you followed me anyway.
You made a bed for us in the woods.
There were sycamore boughs overhead.

Stop there. Stop now. I calculated that
the number of birds singing
on any given morning
was a function of the sycamores plus my hangover.

I said, *Stop there,* but you followed me
even when I tore our bed to pieces,
I did that, I brought anger into the bower
and the sycamores became menacing shoulders.

And the birds cried, scared, a little embarrassed.
And we paced back and forth, under
the menacing shoulders of the sycamores.
The birds made nests inside our heads.

When you held my fist between your two hands,
I pretended to be subdued. But then
I opened my fist easily
and scattered your strength all over the bower.

When you ran towards me, I said, *Stop there,*
stop now, you'll end up
in a stranger's life; and when you ran away
I said the same words over again, louder.

PASTORAL

The woodpecker flew to the woodpile, pecked and fled.
The fox hid. The dog begged. The squirrel slept.
Nobody saw what the child did, silent, behind his book.

Out in the road, headlights were a hard metaphor,
everywhere passing, spot, spot: why do
the neighbors claim to "adore all things Malaysian"?

You could date their house to another century,
give it an obsolete use, an obsolete industry,
say a lathe-making shop or a barn for threshing.

You could see the title on the child's book. But
what made the fox stay hid, the bird stay fled,
what held the sadness animal outdoors all night?

POEM BEGINNING WITH A LINE FROM FROST

as if regret were in it and were sacred
    as if regret itself were a river and want

that was the source of the river flowed
    through the river, more and more the more

the river thickened towards the boring lake
    where what stirred once went terribly quiet.

This is indistinguishable from happiness.
    This standing water was a mindful current once.

Once was a mindful current: now leaden, still;
    it is ourselves we most resemble, now. Now

the maples that had been nowhere gather. When
    we look down what we look down on is our own.

ROMANCE

After *The Winter's Tale*

I scorned you, and when you begged for mercy, I banished you.
Scorning, begging, banishing—that's what the script said.
My life was tragic, was the plot. Disaster sought me out.

Onstage, it was different. I packed your lunch;
I dropped you off, with a playful pat on the ass.
I made sure you saw me glance, once, in the rearview mirror

where I could see you showing me you saw me glance, once.
The night before, we'd partied on a rented tugboat
drifting down the narrow river: from the shore, smooth jazz

was heard between the surges of an ancient outboard motor.
Strangers on the shore guessed, correctly, someone had retired.
The microphone carried the tones, only the tones, of his

sentimental, endless *vale*. Then laughter, then more smooth jazz.
But now my radio told of a dire national emergency:
panic; folk forms of prophecy: omens, conspiracies.

Someone hung up the river, like a long dress on a hanger.
It touched the sky, then fell to the cement, as if the hanger
suddenly snapped. The radio was aghast and hysterical.

And so disaster happened offstage, to others. I was spared.
In Shakespeare when you are banished, time stops for you.
Years later, when you reappeared, you were my daughter's age.

FOUR HORACES

I. *To Dan Chiasson Concerning Fortune*

Far out in the gray waters there are storms, there are crews
in trouble right now, as I write this, as you read this
letter or poem or whatever it is they drown, listen Dan,

the shoreline is no safe harbor either, its sharp rocks
rip even the stoutest hull like it's a wasp's nest
and the wasps swarm the shore, forget the shore, Dan;

oh and Dan, forget that big house inland, that house was built
with envy, not wood, not brick, not stone; it is hell
also to be under the tall tree when the storm rolls in,

leaves fill the air and eddy everywhere, there is no shelter
when the tower falls and the little city surrounding
cries "Eek!" and they start unzipping body bags pronto.

Oh, love is a yo-yo: when you're high, you're already
feeling the pull of gravity, but when you're low,
it's really magical how you climb up the way you fell.

I've made my heart so calloused I can't be cheered,
but you know, Dan, I'm never lonely, and that's something.
In the winter, I don't shiver, I just sit there smiling.

In the summer, I never smile—I play cards indoors.
Apollo isn't always throwing darts, you know—
he has a lyre too and he likes to throw lyre parties.

It's sunny somewhere, Dan. The sun is shining somewhere.

II. *To Helena Concerning Dan Chiasson*

The water at the bottom of the river, way down, the coldest
darkest water: if that water were your only drinking water
what would you do: thirst forever? Or drink the freezing water?

If A, send me a postcard from la-la land, where
Mom bays like a donkey and Dad is an oil slick,
because that's where dehydration takes you, fast.

If B, I'd buy the biggest wool parka I could find
and put it where the sun don't shine—otherwise
you'll feel a subzero chill no mug of tea will thaw.

I chose B, and now it's winter, and I'm outside your door
like a baby seal on an ice island, waiting
to be clubbed or saved by a Green New Zealander.

Come out. When Dan beats off again, when
he drifts away the way he always does, come out:
zip up that pantsuit and rescue me from my Horatian

sense of humor! There's a great jazz bar nearby
that doesn't charge a cover. They will play
only the nine jazz songs we know, over and over.

And the world will narrow the way it always does
when we're together, only nine jazz songs
ever written, and we know every one by heart.

And if some kid from the local jazz college walks in
and starts playing the tenth song, that's when
we get our clubs and club him like a baby seal.

III. *After Party*

Helena, when you froth with the names of stars
I wonder is it a star's kiss, a star's trace
from last night's after party that perplexes me?

You can't buy the tears that adorn my eyes
on eBay or in the diamond district. Those
bruises on you aren't temporary henna tattoos.

Some star put them there after the after party,
before you made him taste the back of your throat.
I know what happens at those after parties, where

Absolut sponsors everything. Everyone puts a drop
of honey somewhere up inside their body and
the game is, where is it, who can find my honey drop?

Meanwhile, where is your Horace? Home, as usual,
translating Dan Chiasson's
petty agonies into his frantic, ancient Latin.

IV. *Peeled Horse*

Helena, now that you have moved away
to a patrician county in New Jersey,
there's a horse under your ass, where I once was.

I would like to make that horse into
an anatomical drawing of himself, all
bone and tissue and staring eye sockets.

I've studied the masters: Battista Franco's
cabinets of femurs and knees, and
the banana-peel exposed skulls of Lucas Kilian—

how would you like to ride that peeled horse,
its bone saddle rattling all day, turning
your ass to bone in the New Jersey afternoon?

TULIP TREE

Out late and the night is a ruin, my voice says
the night is a ruin, my voice doesn't say a thing,
my poem says my voice doesn't say a thing,

your voice says my poem says my voice
doesn't say a thing. Your parents own the tulip tree
we lie under, but they don't own the night.

Nobody does, not even taxpayers! That's why
instead of overhearing a guitar or, from behind curtains,
watching people change, instead of telling stories

I "obsess," as you say, about my tone of voice.
People change. Sometimes at night, curtains drawn,
they turn infinite upon each other, just for fun.

I want fried clams, the ones with gritty fat bellies.
If I strike the apocalyptic tone you like, won't you
drive up Route 1 with me, right now, to find those clams?

MADE-UP MYTH

In the story of the bees, the lovers fall asleep
as flowers and wake as flesh, human flesh
stung so deep, so many times, it hurts the bone.

The way a wheel turns in space, in place,
over and over and gets nowhere—
with agony added, that's what the lovers feel.

Scholars translate the inscription above their bodies,
Beware—my body is spoiled meat, my spit
will parch you, it will never be your sweet milk.

They are made of such strange wishes. Once
he cupped a bee inside his bare palms
on a dare, and felt it slowly electrocute itself.

They are made of such strange dreams, bee-like dreams:
a peach orchard she never played in as a child,
where overnight the peaches never turned to stone.

Who slept as a wildflower, slept as a metaphor,
wakes to feel real pain, the scholars say,
even as the lovers writhe forever in myth-land.

Scholars, if they go down to the riverbank, under
the anchorage, you know the spot, if the lovers
lie down together there, will they wake as flowers?

LOVE SONG (TOLL)

It was near dawn. That night I'd
memorized Raleigh's poem
"Nature, That Washed Her Hands in Milk."

Milk. Jelly. Light. Shit. Dust.
Time that doth not wash
his hands, time that is rust . . .

The bridges and the rivers
they spanned began
trying to begin to shine, as from within.

Near dawn. But when I thought
of all the possible bodies sleeping
in possible apartments, I got into my car

later or earlier than ever before,
later or earlier than ever before
paid the toll-taker my handful of glimmering change.

The road from here to there goes on forever.
Miles pass without a single
notable billboard. The toll-taker, smaller, smaller, vanishes.

I drove through dawn. Miles, then hundreds of miles,
passed, and still the same dull low-slung
sun, the moon behind a gunnysack curtain.

When I climbed into bed beside you it was
still dawn, and it is still dawn
now I've driven back home. You could be anyone.

II. Natural History

In Africa, I saw once with my own eyes a most amazing thing—
a bridegroom turn into a bride upon the altar.

—Pliny,
Natural History, Book IV

The Eye is not satisfied with seeing,
nor the Ear filled with hearing.

—Ecclesiastes 1:8

I. THE SUN

There is one mind in all of us, one soul,
      who parches the soil in some nations

but in others hides perpetually behind a veil;
      he spills light everywhere, here he spilled

some on my tie, but it dried before dinner ended.
      He is in charge of darkness also, also

in charge of crime, in charge of the imagination.
      People fucking flick him off and on,

off and on, with their eyelids as they ascertain
      with their eyes their love's sincerity.

He makes the stars disappear, but he makes
      small stars everywhere, on the hoods of cars,

in the compound eyes of skyscrapers or in the eyes
      of sighing lovers bored with one another.

Onto the surface of the world he stamps
      all plants and animals. They are not gods

but he made us worshippers of every
    bramble toad, black chive, we find.

In Idaho there is a desert cricket that makes
    a clocklike tick-tick when he flies, but he

is not a god. The only god is the sun,
    our mind—master of all crickets and clocks.

II. THE ELEPHANT

How to explain my heroic courtesy? I feel
        that my body was inflated by a mischievous boy.

Once I was the size of a falcon, the size of a lion,
        once I was not the elephant I find I am.

My pelt sags, and my master scolds me for a botched
        trick. I practiced it all night in my tent, so I was

somewhat sleepy. People connect me with sadness
        and, often, rationality. Randall Jarrell compared me

to Wallace Stevens, the American poet. I can see it
        in the lumbering tercets, but in my mind

I am more like Eliot, a man of Europe, a man
        of cultivation. Anyone so ceremonious suffers

breakdowns. I do not like the spectacular experiments
        with balance, the high-wire act and cones.

We elephants are images of humility, as when we
        undertake our melancholy migrations to die.

Did you know, though, that elephants were taught
        to write the Greek alphabet with their hooves?

Worn out by suffering, we lie on our great backs,
        tossing grass up to heaven—as a distraction, not a prayer.

That's not humility you see on our long final journeys:
        it's procrastination. It hurts my heavy body to lie down.

III. PURPLE BUSH

The whiff of an extinguished candle
     will sometimes cause a miscarriage.

Eels must travel far upstream to where
     the river becomes a ribbon to spawn.

In that shallow water their babies risk
     exposure to the harsh midday sun.

Seeing a blind man in the ninth month
     can result in babies born without faces.

Their nurses use rare dyes to paint
     nearly permanent eyes and noses

on these featureless babies, but the use
     of such dyes causes sterility in women.

A sterile woman is a plague on armies.
     Whole armies have been slaughtered

for the barrenness of one soldier's wife.
     If the soldier lives, he's stoned to death or hanged.

Wade deep into the woods, go far from home,
        you will find a purple bush. The berries

of this bush bring perfect health, but health
        stirs envy, and envy makes the neighbor a killer.

IV. THE HYENAS

Picture a house in a storybook. It is some color
        houses never are—sky blue, or fire-engine red.

The winding trail that leads to its front door is
        crisscrossed by trees. But when you turn the page

the undulating hills around the little house
        begin to fill with voices. These voices cannot

be drawn. You must imagine the voices, because
        the little people in the storybook cannot hear;

they are cartoons. You thought you were an ignorant
        cartoon, but part of what these voices are saying

is that you are not, come out, come out. In some
        legends they know your name, and say it sweetly;

in others they coo like doves or whine like
        injured dogs. As you stare at the page, the house,

the trees, the voices grow louder, saying come out,
        come out; now they are everywhere, the way water

is everywhere when you are underwater.
        On the last page of the storybook the people

look sad, but it is not because the storybook
        is over. They live in there. It was a momentary

catastrophe. But you will never again live happily
        in your house, its acres and acres of silence.

V. THE BEAR

In quiet, in the exquisite privacy of a cave, a bear
      gives birth. Outside the cave it's rain, a driving rain,

but inside there is no sound, only the thump-thump
      of her convulsing body and her babies' cries.

Her cubs are white screaming lumps, eyeless until
      she licks their eyes into place, bald until

she paints fur up and down their bodies with her tongue.
      It is a litter of five, at least; it is hard to see

how many have burrowed under her soft belly.
      Also, this is ancient Rome; it is hard to see through

so much time. It makes you wonder how many
      other beautiful sights are hidden away in time,

a cavelike element noted for its dimness. Now she
      and her cubs are emerging from the cave, leaving

one weakling behind. He is lame, and will not survive
      this rainy night two thousand years ago. By now

he is vanishing into the floor of the dark cave,
　　　　even his newly painted fur, even his fresh eyes.

By now he's gone entirely from view.
　　　　All the caves on this hill are identical again.

VI. FROM THE LIFE OF GORKY

Thinking of the local murdered girl, the news, her hose, and the word "holler" (*She hollered,* said the dishwasher who'd been released, of course, earlier that summer), I read the first chapter of Gorky's *My Childhood*.

*

Gorky's father's corpse is on the kitchen floor, his mother combing her husband's hair, when suddenly she hollers *Jesus!,* writhing on the cold floor there, beside the body.

*

What happens next, you won't believe—she gives birth, propped up against her husband's corpse, right there in chapter one of Gorky's memoir.

*

Gorky's little brother hollers his first cries.

*

It's gotten late.

*

I'm reading in the dark.

VII. GEORGIC

Whether to twine the flowers around the maples, whether
      the chipped antler found in the sod portend a hot summer,

whether a hot summer portend interiors fogged by breath,
      reeking of sweat and shit, and can the hoe save us,

and can the spade, and if we pot the peach pit
      in a terra-cotta pot, will we have peaches next year?

Will we have peaches ever? If the clouds overhead
      spell *Angie and Ed,* have we seen something spectacular?

Is there a pilot somewhere with an agile plane who'll write
      what we say in the sky? *I wish I were a tree,* wrote Herbert,

for sure then I should come to fruit or shade—what use,
      the pulse that makes the poem race weakens me, *what use,*

I found a shriveled cherry and a shrimp tail in my
      suit pocket, I never wear it, it hangs in the closet.

My forehead is blank like the sky and good for writing.
      Sparrow, make your nest in me, come down from the sky.

VIII. PLINY

I stepped on a bird this morning. It had fallen between
      two parked cars. My boot heel made it make a quiet,

sobbing noise, not at all like birdsong. It was
      brittle and soft at once, like matchsticks inside

chewing gum. As a child in Rome, I dreamed someday
      I would be Emerson's "transparent eyeball." I tried

different ways to disappear: I wore a football helmet
      everywhere. What I found out was: you can't

be a transparent eyeball in a football helmet.
      I feel better in the dark. I compare the dark

to chocolate: some rich, naughty substance covering
      my body. That would be invisible—to be dipped in chocolate.

That's no football helmet. What if pain turned
      the bird inside out, what if its own scale were volcanic?

You've got to get yourself dirty to imagine it.
      You've got to get down on all fours and bark.

IX. FROM THE LIFE OF GORKY (II)

I am on a hill near Nizhniy. The time is dawn. It is 1880.

That outline is a constable.

That is his splattering boots.

We're here to bury my father: why else would those spades be stuck in a loam pile?

Now he blows a whistle, shouts, *Hurry up!*

The wind dies, and the weeping increases.

*

We're in a time of incessant action, up/down up/down. The pile shrinks as the sun rises.

*

Now it is morning in New York City, and I've made a gross discovery: my kosher salt is full of something's larvae.

Why would you lay your eggs in salt? Can anyone tell me, what kind of creature leaves its babies behind in a box of salt?

*

Now it is morning over Nizhniy.

*

My father's canary-yellow coffin is already a memory.

X. THE ELEPHANT (II)

The others were baited with serene, contented elephants,
    brought indoors for the first time ever, given

barley juice and honey poured from the skull of a monkey.
    But what they did to me—it fills me with weird shame.

It's worse than when I got drunk at the department party
    and showed off that photograph of my anus. Worse than

when I was caught masturbating at the Laundromat.
    In Ethiopia, you see, I'm all the meat there is. He waited

in the bole of the tree, keeping a lookout for me,
    the only laggard. I read that Stevens was like me,

a slow, methodical walker. It is left to later generations
    to draw the line where daydream, revery, etc., end and

"great poetry" begins. He rode atop my right haunch,
    holding on to my tail. When his ax struck, it was

so warm at first, I thought I'd pissed my pants.
    I had not pissed my pants. I had a mouthful of dirt.

XI. MAKING PURPLE

Nibble what nibbles you, play dead, play bored;
    play sad, shell gaping, like the cockle used for bait;

like the melting purple eat the mud, be seen through
    like the pebble purple, soft like the reef purple.

Imagine yourself suffusing a woman's gown or sheets
    your bloodstream running through her inkwell.

Those rich dyes once were your ideas, your love
    of broccoli rabe. Half-killed cockles attract purples,

the reef is littered with open mouths waiting to snap.
    I am trying to make my pain attractive, my yearning

pretty. A man caught me in a fine-ply lobster pot.
    He scalded me until I nearly died, then threw me back.

I gape like this because of the ordeal. Did you foresee
    this moment, where what you intended to devour

devours you? Did you know they'd haul us up
    into the suffocating air, our bodies fused together?

XII. PLINY (II)

I became a tiny eye to see into the eye of a sparrow,
    a cricket's eye, a baby's eye; when I looked

at the night sky, I made my eye as big as history, for
    the night sky is a kaleidoscope of past times,

as noted astronomer Carl Sagan said. I watched TV and
    made my eye a TV: lidless, rash gazer at whatever happens,

casting shadows of what happens for the neighbors,
    whose eyes are the size of windows, my windows, and sharpen

their sight to voluptuous desire, voyeur voyeur
    pants on fire. Anything half-seen becomes what's on,

becomes the neighbors' newscast, lotto drawing, rerun.
    How do you know a child has died except by watching

trays of casseroles brought in, the old sit-down,
    peoples' bodies doing as bodies will against the wall?

XIII. INSCRIBED ON A LINTEL

I was born beside a quarry. I played in granite
    spray and gravel, dust up to my elbows.

I was born beside the ocean, I played in the tide,
    at night I sucked my arm to get the salt out.

I was born beside a mountain, I played under
    evergreens. At night my life seemed haunted.

I lived beside a quarry, I worked deep in the earth,
    I made my body a drill to burrow into stone.

I lived beside the ocean, I worked inside the water,
    I made my body a net and I cast myself wide.

I lived beside a mountain, I worked inside the wood,
    I made my body a saw and I cleared a field.

All my life when I worked, I disappeared inside
    my work; so when my work ended, I disappeared.

XIV. NEWS

The news on the forgotten friend is not good, no
    not at all: his head is swelling up, but inside,

where there's no room left. Outside, America is empty—
    spilled towns, old industries, territories spiky

with wildflowers, the sky is a pile of air, even
    the ocean is a possible frontier, and still his head

decides to grow in the wrong direction. It changes
    colors as you drive west, O it goes green to

brown, brown to red, red to green, and the West
    is just like the movies, cacti flower there.

Would you ever drive across America for a friend,
    would you watch canyons pass, plains, mountains

pass, would you drive that far for any reason
    but to see a girl, preferably a near stranger?

XV. RANDALL JARRELL

I've never written in a way that really pleases Dan.
    His opinion is invaluable to me, but I am shy—

so shy I left the earth five years or so before
    he arrived. He likes "90 North," I know—

and the Rilke poem whose title he can't presently recall.
    I did that one with him in mind. A corpse is stiff,

its arms extended like a man giving "commandments."
    Of course the dead do command us, in their way.

For example: reread my last book, *The Lost World.*
    Now compare my boyhood in L.A. to Dan's:

read his first book, *The Afterlife of Objects*.
    He tried on the confessional style for a while.

If people hurt you, tell on them: perhaps you'll heal.
    If language hurts you, make the damage real.

What else? A poem about a hopping toad should never be
    an allegory for epistemology or Wittgenstein.

Read Proust for soft focus. Read Rilke for nostalgia.
    Richard Wilbur was the future once, but weren't we all?

XVI. THE PIGEON

Once startled, you shall feel hours of weird sadness
    afterwards. This is known as the rule of the pigeon.

This is the rule of the Herbert scholar: your head
    shall come to rest in a Ziploc terrarium, not a park.

You shall be feted in the pages of *New York* magazine,
    and at department meetings, over eggnog, mourned.

This is the rule of the girl you loved: you shall heave
    and heave all night, alone, and not from love, not

from anything like love. Peel that mattress off your back,
    but peel you never will the remorse-stain, and

this is the rule of The Who, you shall be Muzak,
    you shall be orchestral, electronic and franchised.

You shall be blood, is the rule of the sleepless night,
    and you shall be drained of blood, is the rule of dawn.

The scholar and the pigeon shall inhabit the same street,
    your street, but you shall remember the pigeon longer.

XVII. THE ELEPHANT (III)

When he hit me square on the head I said *Better to die*
    this way than in obscurity, on the empty plain.

A heron and a hawk, a monkey carrying a monkey skull,
    a lion on fire and a pack of eyeless wolves

were what I feared, my rib cage rocking to and fro
    in the sun, in the wind, all day and night, a dinghy

anchored in rough seas. Not this: my body a sack of
    garbage, hooves bound, the world turned upside down.

This is a beautiful country, said John Brown on his way
    to the gallows, *I have not cast my eyes o'er it before—*

that is, in this direction. And I said, *What a beautiful banquet,*
    I am honored to contribute. They cleaned my skull

with pulverized mica for their cornucopia: those were
    my eye sockets overflowing with black grapes, herrings

lying in piles of their own, jewel-like, dewlike roe
    made the crown of my head, and the bride was beautiful.

XVIII. "THERE IS A STAR IN THE SEA"

Pliny, *Natural History,* Book IX

"There is a star in the sea, and it burns up everything
    it touches. Though men who walk on land deny it,

one night a star fell from the sky and landed in the sea.
    It had the good sense to become a fish, but the wit

to keep its shape. It sleeps on the bottom of the sea,
    but one day I'll play a trick on it—I'll turn the ocean

upside down! Then it will shine again, coral bluff,
    rusted galleon in the night sky, and I will pray to it."

XIX. GEORGIC (II)

The flowers that fade, the flowers that don't, the wax
    begonias made to look like real ones by an artisan in

Quebec, the wax insects that buzz nearby and the wax fragrance
    that attracts them, the wax lovers walking idly, their

wax promises, the entire scene done in a shoe box with a peephole
    to grant the wax lovers privacy, making your looking,

your mere looking, forbidden and therefore wonderful—
    what was that again, listen—this wax man and woman,

what disappointment is it now bows him down, as she
    half-comforts him, while her other half makes a call

on a cell phone? The flowers beam anyway, clueless.
    They ignore us—if what I mean by "us" is the wax lovers,

you and I, making a fetish of our privacy again, putting joy
    in someone's eye. And that's what I mean by us.

XX. THINGS I SAW WITH MY OWN EYES

I saw a stout man turn into a bird, then shed
    his feathers, one by one, and become a woman.

I saw a hippocentaur preserved in honey, wheeled
    through town by a bellowing entrepreneur.

On a feast day, a man lay down upon the banquet
    and spewed forth sweet wine from his genitals.

It soaked everyone's clothes and stained our skin—
    hilarity ensued, until the wine turned to blood.

When we were soaked with his blood, the man died.
    There was chaos in the hall, and much howling.

Tribes in India howl when they are happy. I saw
    a woman give birth to a hundred children,

like drops from a dripping faucet or luggage on
    a luggage carousel. If you are perfectly still

and you lie down in a field, soon your body
    will be covered by sparrows, but move an inch

and they fly away all at once, leaving you naked,
    and scatter everywhere above you in the sky.

XXI. FROM THE LIFE OF GORKY (III)

On the boat I ate watermelons and cantaloupe in secret. There was a man on board, forever drunk, dressed like a policeman, who forbade the eating of fruit. If you got caught with fruit, he scolded you and threw it in the river. This he called his "wild justice."

*

Was it justice when, one night, approaching shore, he threw himself overboard?

*

More vodka for Grandmother. Another of her saint-devoured-by-a-wild-beast stories.

*

In a corner of the cabin, wrapped in a white sheet tied with a bright red ribbon, my newborn brother Maxim—who caught death, Mother said, from his father's dead hand.

*

A storm. Rainwater whips the horse's eye of the porthole I look out from.

*

When my uncle said, *Alexei, why do you cry?* I answered, *For Maxim: the storm tosses him to and fro.*

XXII. THE BURIAL OF CHILDREN

Children buried in pairs, twins buried in a single coffin,
    their arms entwined, or wrapped in one white sheet;

children buried with curios and whatnots, pictures
    of themselves as infants, their pets killed and buried

beside them; lacquered with honey, with lemonade,
    spearmint children, lavender and thyme children,

a goldenrod crown for the golden boy, wheat and whey
    and cornstalks for the farmer's girl, and some children

were buried in large glass jars. Fucking fly laid its eggs
    in my box of salt, and a girl I know misplaced her baby,

now every baby she sees she thinks it's hers. Children
    were buried in large glass jars, bent fetus-like

at the neck at the waist at the knees at the toes as though
    the glass were that sweet fluid they first breathed.

Be careful what you love, what you presume to love.
    Who suckles salt, with the sticky honey jar nearby?

XXIII. WHICH SPECIES ON EARTH IS SADDEST?

When we wake up in our bodies, first we weep.
        We weep because the air is thick as honey.

Even the air is a body. Ours is the bottommost
        and newest body, nested inside other, older ones

(though the mother's body is repairing itself now;
        there's no trace of us anywhere on her;

why are we part of every body but our mother's?)
        Die as soon as possible, the Scriptures say.

And many do—or soon enough, as in the tales of
        a swollen boy, now years ago, in farthest Africa,

who filled a grove of cherry trees with tears, then
        vanished into the grove. He hides behind trees.

That's death for you, a fragrant grove to hide within,
        your sister looking for you in a pile of cocaine.

That's weeping for you. Grief is a cherry grove.
        Don't be born at all. My friend is on fast-forward now

to reach the scene where they erase her childlessness.
     She knows she hid that kid somewhere inside of her,

but where? We know nothing else except by learning:
     not walking, not eating. Only to cry comes naturally.

XXIV. THE SOIL

Stay whole, stay full, stay mild: the soil absorbs
      whatever falls: apple, animal, apple-pie wrapper.

Anywhere on earth you go, get yourself full on
      other people's mothers, other people's sweethearts.

Drought come, flood you with new food. Cancer riff,
      cancer chafe and giggle, soil stay full.

Upholstery swallow you, you stay full. Roast
      destroy your muscle, you stay mild. Wall-to-wall

cover you, you stay whole: you're wall-to-wall on earth.
      My mother ached for weeks, then blossomed into

a pain petunia. The president's head wound is on rewind.
      Over and over the skyscraper zips and unzips.

Now I am famous in the world of arts and letters
      many Internet entries are me, many are not—

there's my name on the official embalmers' site, but
      that's not me answering the Q&A. Someday

I will be the Q&A on the embalmers' site, but
        if the arithmetic holds, I'll beat the embalmer.

The sweetheart and the mother disappear, but
        everybody here is present and accounted for.

My girl malignant cries that she used to be benign;
        my neighbor wheelchair was a volleyball champion.

Stay whole, stay full, stay mild: the world is a cradle—
        no, a wheelbarrow. It hauls shit and dirt and hay.

III.

It is known that one elephant, who was
rather slow in learning his tricks and
had been punished severely by his
master's beating, was discovered later
that night, alone in his tent, practicing
those tricks.

—Pliny,
Natural History, Book VIII

"SCARED BY THE SMALLEST SHRIEK OF A PIG, AND WHEN WOUNDED, ALWAYS GIVE GROUND."

What we saw on festival day: play infantries
with real spears, real veins, a real soldier
pulled across the festival grounds trailing blood
the way a paintbrush is pulled across a canvas;
lesser mischief, on the periphery: my friend saw
a man gouge out an elephant's eyes with a shovel,
and the elephant cried, *Oh, Murder, I am Murdered!*
the way we do—wordless, comical, like a choir of kazoos:

is that poetry? Or is poetry picking the scarcest word,
say, "charred" instead of "burned"—
as in "charred in a fire"? Real life is so raw,
all on its own; it hurts; words should perhaps
protect us from real life.
Perhaps words should be a shield, rather than
a mirror; and maybe poems should be
an ornamented shield, like the shields

gods made for their favorite soldiers,
sons and lovers. Poems should be
like people's faces by firelight:
a little true, for verification's sake,
but primarily beautiful. Or like
pomegranates: hard to open at first
but, when you get them open, full of sweet granules
of meaning. Once, when I was bathed in wine

as part of a military victory parade,
I was purple for a month—
I liked the looks of me that way,
like a giant pomegranate seed!
That's what a poem should be:
recognizable reality, but dyed,
a sign that someone here felt joy,
someone was released from pain,

one minute he lived he felt no pain,
the war was over, killing was over
and he was not killed, not maimed.
I liked myself that way. I remember
as a boy, after she had done her obsequies
to the moon, down at the riverbank,
my mother put me to bed and whispered,
"Frederick"—for that is my name—"Frederick,

you saved my life; Mommy wanted to die
before she felt you stir inside her."
It made me feel wonderful. Thereafter,
I never felt anything other
than completely central to her life—
what a gift that was. I suppose I understand
my future years in light of our intense
bond, my hours waiting for her outside

the dispatcher's office, the time she
dated a guy with a criminal record
and soon she found out why—I held her
that time, that time she was the calf
and I the mommy. She was a kind of guitar
to learn forgiveness on, its harmonies
and, yes, even its bungled chords.
And I learned to pity the powerful—

my trainer, forcing me to puff a cigarette,
was himself forced, by powers
far greater than he, to force me;
so I did it, though my lungs hurt,
though my lungs felt sandpapered after.
I almost wrote "sadpapered" there; isn't it weird
the way the mind works, because
as I fill this paper up with words

I do feel sad, thinking of him lighting
that cigarette, placing it between my lips,
the wild applause, our strange
intimacy, and my relief—my God,
I thought I might swallow
that fire and become fire. Let me tell you
about my sister, Sarah, and a custom
that's long since been lost: Sarah

was hired to be a lying-in girl
by the Bridgeport Circus. This was before
the war, or rather, between them.
The ringmaster, not yet famous, invented
a new high-wire act: a large bull
would carry a petite cow across
the wire, holding her in a bonnet
hung upon his trunk, the cow lying

in a pile of down blankets, moaning.
The crowd was stunned: never
had they seen an elephant carry
another elephant across the sky,
across the almost invisible single thread
of twine. Once the bull crossed
and backed down the ladder, though—
surprise! From the bonnet, a pair of calves

appear and sport around the ring!
"Lying-in Sarah" made the circus rich.
The ultimate fate of that circus need not
here be discussed: that fire was
a tragedy, just let me say; and say also,
it was *not* Mother's fault. Sarah's
memorabilia are strewn all over
my apartment; someday I'll frame it all;

someday the world will know
her name and perhaps associate me
with her in some small way. I am aware
that in certain uncivilized places,
where men grunt at one another
and know not speech, know not poetry
or any other art that ennobles us,
elephants still are hunted for their tusks;

myself, I had my own removed as soon
as I had the money, and hired
an artisan to carve from them my life's story—
there is an icon of the moon; a river
icon; three figures together, representing
Sarah, my mother and me; a flag
to show my love of country . . .
but I've gone on too long. And plus,

the things people accumulate and say
"This was my life"—it isn't just boring,
it's also vaguely creepy, even if it was
once part of their bodies. Is it this way
with poetry? I hope not, since all day long
I write my poetry, my "sadpaper."
Let others say if I'm bronze or not, say
if this Frederick be a poet or a scribbler.

Notes

My title refers to Pliny the Elder's *Historia Naturalis,* which I first encountered after reading Italo Calvino's essay on it, "Man, the Sky, and the Elephant." The poems in the title sequence and the longer poem that closes the book derive elements in their stance, their voice, and their cadence from Pliny. In a very few cases, as in "The Elephant (I)," I have borrowed images and phrases from Pliny as well.

The lines attributed to John Brown in "The Elephant (III)" were brought to my attention by Forrest Gander's book *Torn Awake,* where they serve as an epigraph. The poems about Gorky borrow ideas from Maxim Gorky's *My Childhood.* The line from Frost that opens "Poem Beginning with a Line from Frost" is from "West-Running Brook," and was suggested to me by Desales Harrison. The Horaces in Section I are composites of things I found in the odes of Horace and things I made up. These poems are indebted to David Ferry, whose translations of Horace formed totally my imagination of the Roman poet.

—D.C.

A NOTE ABOUT THE AUTHOR

Dan Chiasson was born in Burlington, Vermont, and was educated at Amherst College and Harvard University, where he completed a Ph.D. in American poetry. His first book of poems, *The Afterlife of Objects*, was published in 2002 by the University of Chicago Press, and a book of criticism, *One of Everything: Post-war American Poetry and Experience* was published by Chicago in 2007. Chiasson is the recipient of a Pushcart Prize, a Whiting Fellowship in the Humanities, and also a Whiting Writers' Award. He teaches at Wellesley College.

A NOTE ABOUT THE TYPE

This book was set in Cushing, a font named after J. Stearns Cushing, the Boston-based book printer who created the typeface in a roman weight for the American Type Founders in 1897. A few years later, in 1904, Frederic Goudy added an italic version. The typeface was revived in 1982, when the International Typeface Corporation and designer Vincent Pacella added more weights and transformed the design to its present state—slightly condensed, bracketed serifs—thus creating a complete family for this "Egyptian" font.

Composed by Creative Graphics,
Allentown, Pennsylvania

Printed and bound by Thomson-Shore,
Dexter, Michigan

Designed by Soonyoung Kwon